What If . . .

53 MEDITATIONS
OF THE SOUL

by Waceke Wambaa

All images courtesy of the Author.

Library of Congress Cataloging-in-Publication Data

Names: Wambaa, Waceke, 1974- author
Title: What If... 53 Meditations of the Soul / Waceke Wambaa

ISBN: (print/hardcover) 979-8-9882579-0-5
ISBN: (ebook) 979-8-9882579-1-2
ISBN: (audiobook) 979-8-9882579-2-9

Subjects: Mental health | Wellness | Meditation
Book Cover by Waceke Wambaa
First Edition 2023

Published by TataCeke Publishing
victoriousthinking.com
wacekewambaa.com

For my family—for all the times you've caused me to agitate, meditate, regurgitate, accommodate, ruminate, contemplate, appropriate, and every other -ate that begs to be emotionally noticed. I wouldn't trade you for anything . . . I think.

CONTENTS

THE PURPOSE

Wait a minute! Here's someone else talking about meditation . . . why should I lend my ears, eyes, or brain cells to this endeavor?

Gosh! Let's face it, at some point I've asked myself the same question. Like, even, "What's meditation and why should I do whatever meditation actually is?"

Good point! Truthfully, numerous definitions abound on meditation—circling in on the idea of repetition, practice, focusing our thoughts, clearing our minds to have uninterrupted study of something, someone, an idea, activity, etc. This is for the purpose of improved objectivity and well-being of ourselves and the situations we may find ourselves in.

While it sounds like easy enough of a concept, the reality is because we human beings are such complex entities with seemingly infinitesimal possibilities, meditation as a practice, with all its variations, becomes something not as simple and straightforward to do.

Yet in our stressed out, upside down, inside out world, the documented and purported benefits of meditation are not to be taken lightly when they positively affect the quality of our lives.

Why meditate?

We meditate because the benefits of honest and effectual meditation help you and me in our journey toward living out our created potential. These benefits are numerous and well documented as an effective tool in reducing stress, helping promote emotional health, control anxiety, improve attention span, improve self-awareness, better our coping skills, improve sleep, help decrease blood pressure, and more.

Back to this book . . . why bother reading it?

What If . . . 53 Meditations of the Soul is specifically designed to help you in your journey toward meaningful and effective meditation by providing a well thought out yet simple and practical tool toward this journey. It provides meditation points that at some point in our lives we have consciously or unconsciously touched upon. This book offers an easy-to-understand meditation framework within which to ponder these and any other points or experiences you might find yourself in.

There are no abstract formulas or items to purchase or places to be in order to step into this meditation journey. Just bring yourself and a space, a place where you can be you, uninterrupted, for a brief moment in time and meditate.

If you're wondering if this book is really for you, let me start by asking you these questions:

- Do you want to know more about meditation and wish someone would provide an easy to understand framework on how to effectively meditate?
- Perhaps you have had scattered thoughts and been distracted? Where you wish you could learn strategies on how to focus, especially when it negatively impacts the quality of your life.
- How about the "S" word . . . stress? Do you find that when you stress out, it's not easy reigning in that stress?
- Speaking of stress, have you seen or heard local and international news lately? Everything is so unsettled. Have you found yourself looking for ways to be able to process this information or find peace in the midst of all the angst?

- Are you are looking for an easily digestible meditation resource for you, and one you can share with others in a way that invites conversation, contemplation, and more?

If this is you, please read on, as this book is designed with you in mind! It will help you:

- Learn how to get rid of distractions
- Develop a stronger identity and belief in yourself
- Develop good habits, break your bad habits
- Learn a strategy on how to quiet your thoughts
- Make small changes that deliver big life changing results

My hope is that by sharing *What If . . . 53 Meditations of the Soul* with you, you'll find yourself taking one step closer to living out your created potential.

Welcome.

AN INTRODUCTION

What if there's really more than meets the eye?

What if I dare myself to think on the more, to ponder on what's deeper than surface knowledge?

What if I take a good look into the deeper parts of me?

What if I take a deep breath and introduce me to me?

What will I find?

What if?

The premise of this book is simple yet profound. What if—for one minute or more, an hour or more, one day at a time or more, stretching it out for one week, perhaps more—I take one statement. And for a moment in time, I meditate on all the possibilities set before me. In a sense, become a serious ruminator. Now, I'm not talking about focusing on negative or dark situations; rather, chewing on statements designed to encourage self-reflection. Perhaps peel away layers that were initially designed for survival mode, but have long since worn out their welcome. What remains may be a bit murky and sensitive to handle, but could become a catalyst for forging a positive path to ultimately thrive on all levels of one's existence. Let me explain.

First of all, what exactly is a ruminator?

Without getting into deep scientific explanations and definitions (ones I am still on the journey to fully comprehend), for our purposes, a ruminator or "cud-chewer" is a type of mammal with up to four specialized or adapted stomach chambers not available to other animals. These chambers allow for digestion of resources that, while good for ruminant grazing, are not viable or optimal fodder for all mammals. Cattle, sheep, goats, and antelopes are ruminators.

Each chamber of the stomach allows greater nutrient extraction, dependent upon the quality of the food ingested and the time taken to thoroughly digest the food. Thus, during rest periods, the animals will regurgitate "cud"—the previously swallowed food from one of the specialized chambers—to re-chew and break it down (yes, gross, but necessary for our discussion). This allows for the most favorable function of the digestive process: optimizing the health and well-being of that animal.

Why is this important to us?

Well, when we think of "chewing on" or meditating on a bevy of thoughts or ideas, we ruminate. By ruminating on a thought, a belief about ourselves, our circumstances, or lives, we *return* (regurgitate) the idea to the forefront of our conscious minds. It may be a current thought, or for various reasons, one consciously or unconsciously shelved over the course of time.

We turn it around, looking at it from various angles, assessing past, present, and future possible implications, applications, ramifications, and relevance to where we find ourselves in our life's journey.

By intentionally ruminating through using this book, we allow the ideas postulated to be lighthouses we fix our gaze on, or lifeboats to help us—no matter how adrift we find ourselves—on our journey back to the shore and solid ground.

But it can be a fierce battle to engage the heart, a battle just to pry open the door of the mind. Whether it's so painful we don't want to open the said door, or we don't know the existence of a door, or the door is too heavy to operate. Perhaps we intentionally locked the door and have long discarded the key, or we just don't want to use the key in the first place—the battle has many fronts on which to be fought. These battles must be won to ultimately help express the best potential version of ourselves.

What is the battle?

It's the age-old reality of truth battling

the mist-forming, darkness-welcoming

confusions

illusions

delusions

light- and life-stealing ideas

ideals

suggestions and such . . .

that seek to influence, encapsulate, and shackle

who we consciously and subconsciously are

or hope to be.

Thus, when we repeatedly meditate or familiarize ourselves with any thought or idea (whether it's a truth-affirming, life-building idea, or one in opposition to truth), it becomes familiar, acceptable, and ultimately assimilated by us, eventually taking root as a vital component of who we see ourselves to be.

Going back to our ruminators. When they initially encounter food, quantity is the name of the game, not quality. Their focus is on rapid consumption of food during the initial grazing period, so food breakdown for optimal digestion and nutrient extraction is placed on the back burner. Hmmm . . . there is an uncomfortable parallel to be made between the rapid, almost thoughtless consumption of ruminator food ingestion and our lives today. We, too, live in an ever-increasing instantaneous-vacuum-in-anything-on-contact society.

In today's world of quick,
>>*fast,*
>>>>*immediate delivery of life's pleasures and treasures,*
>>>>>*joys and sorrows,*
>>>>>>*inventions and obsoletes,*
>>>>>>>*next-greatest,*
>>>>>>>>*newest,*
>>>>>>>>*fastest,*
>>>>>>>>*influencer,*
>>>>>>>>*youngest,*
>>>>>>>>*strongest,*
>>>>>>>>*richest,*
>>>>>>>>*beautifulest,*
>>>>>>>>*winningest,*
>>>>>>>>*next best thing,*
>>>>>>>>*et cetera, et cetera,*
>*we find that we have allowed a society to flourish that*
increasingly, insatiably gobbles up Every Available Moment of
Our Existence.

We find that we don't have the time to *stop*, to *ponder* the various layers of life hurled at us from all conceivable sources of input. Or maybe this is a lost skill in the fast-paced world we live in.

This 53-point meditation journey attempts to facilitate a slowdown, if you will, for a brief moment in our lives—to consider the "more" of our existence. It provides an opportunity for us to allow ourselves to chew on courage-filled statements and positive ideas that build up the self, and in due course will undoubtedly impact others.

What does the ruminating process entail?

When I say "eat and regurgitate a statement," I mean that I swirl the statement around in the foremost and nether regions of my mind. I let it marinate deep. Real deep. See if I might find an unknown chamber of my heart, hidden and locked away. A chamber I need to open up, dust off, delve into, dig deep, and find what I uncover about myself—*why* the statement being pondered seems to simultaneously be good, bad, and ugly.

Am I able to ask myself honest questions like . . .

Do the points being meditated on resonate positively or negatively deep within me?

Do they cause me to take a hard look inside, to ultimately find I'm able to turn a prior negative perception of myself or my life into a positive one?

Or, perhaps with the aid of a qualified practitioner, can I confront truths or misconceptions of myself and walk in the right direction toward all I was created to be?

By no means does this book postulate to present an exhaustive list of life's deepest issues along with their complete resolution. Rather, this compilation of statements is designed to help you start somewhere.

*So, **what if** you start now?*

A HOW-TO GUIDE

In a nutshell: read–meditate–marinate–consider–read–meditate and marinate some more. You will also find this book provides opportunities for you to create a written history of your meditations as they occur.

Practically, what does this look like?

To start with, each meditation is on its own—this allows for the focal point to be the meditation and the meditation alone. With the two pages following the meditation, you decide how you'd like to explore the given meditation and further document your ruminations.

Some of us are supremely comfortable journaling our ruminations via mental images and pictures judicially stored in the original cloud storage (our brains), with no further need for pen, paper, computer, or otherwise. Others of us might prefer to write, draw, collage, doodle, or some other manner of written recording of our experiences. All options are in play here.

So, whether you're a person who writes out full thoughts in paragraphs, a phrase or a word, or perhaps you're not sure where to start, this book has provided the freedom for you to express yourself as you were created. The space provided in this book is to continue with, enhance, and discover your meditation process as you ruminate, jotting down what you discover in a way that you'll appreciate for the now and in the near and distant future.

Please remember, by no means is this exercise meant to be a rigid experience. Give yourself time to unpack each meditation. It might take you three days on one meditation before you start on the next. Perhaps an hour for one and two weeks for the other. Or you may choose to be systematic and ruminate over each meditation for a week, which will take you through a full year's worth of meditations. This strategy is okay too. No one can set your pace but you.

So no pressure my friend, as you journey through these fifty-three mediations. Do you.

Em, so what's with the pages following each meditation?

Great question! Whether you're a seasoned pro or someone wondering what practical, active meditation looks like, take a relaxing breath and start by throwing out the PhD laundry list of expectations.

Simplicity is key.

This book structures the meditations in two parts. Each meditation is given uncluttered space and stands alone on a page, and following each statement you will find a meditation guideline. The suggested guideline is divided into three sections: "For Real," "Later," and "Step Up 'n' Out," which are detailed below. The space provided gives you the freedom to journal as you choose during each meditation experience—you may use none, some, or all of the space.

When we meditate, there will be thoughts and experiences that inevitably come to mind. But how do we sort them all out? How do we figure out what to focus on, what to dump, or what to save for later? How do we not get overwhelmed or forget an important point that we wanted to look at more closely?

This is where the meditation guideline comes in. It's super handy and simple for providing the space to organize your thoughts and feelings and help you through your meditative process.

Let's go in deeper . . .

The "For Real" Section

This is where the belly of your ruminations find their home. Your focal point.

What is it you're experiencing as you read the meditation? Pay attention to sights, sounds, memories that may arise. Or perhaps a taste rekindled. Jot it all down.

What thoughts come to mind? What thoughts seem highlighted, won't leave, or keep coming up during the course of your ruminations and thereafter? Maybe they don't initially feel connected to the meditation, but you just can't shake off the thoughts hours later. Pay attention here. There may be more than meets the eye. Allow your meditations on vague or highlighted points to simmer like a good stew. Sooner or later, a key point is likely to come into focus.

What about emotions? What are you feeling? What is your pain point, joy point? What has caused you to go "Huh?" or "Aha!"?

All your newfound revelations, confirmations, and such can be recorded in the "For Real" section. Give yourself time to explore the thoughts and feelings, allowing yourself to "let go" and see where your meditations lead you. This could be for a moment, or perhaps hours, or days. You might surprise yourself.

The "Later" Section

Indeed, meditation is also a journey in separating all the external noise and influences and connecting with and within yourself—with who and what you find, your thoughts, the reactions and feelings conveyed as you ponder that thought. To be successful at this endeavor, we have to learn how to systematically delete or at least far remove any competing thought, action, event in our past, present, and future that tend to be at work to diligently confuse and drown out our intended purpose. And by the way, they pop up at the least expected moment. I've learned that sometimes the easiest thing to do is use the word "later" to compartmentalize these distractions, so that I don't spend so much time and energy trying to focus on something I was never meant to focus on.

Thus, when working through these meditations, the distractions you notice popping up can be easily placed in the "Later" section provided. You may find yourself going down the bunny trail of experiences that might be loosely associated with your meditation or not at all. It helps to jot them all down, allowing yourself the grace and space to track one thought, one experience at a time. Over time, this will give you breathing room to further explore what that meditation and its associated experiences mean to you and for you.

So whether it's something practical like recalling a doctor's appointment or as inconsequential as "I wonder how many stripes a zebra has"—they all go in the "Later" section to help declutter our minds and focus on the meditation point of the moment. And yes, later on, one can revisit the list generated and act accordingly. This will better allow you to focus on the "For Real" section and the personal revelations you get from the meditation for as long as you need to. This is not a race, so give yourself the time to unpack it all. Again, "chew your cud."

Intent—when intentionally acted upon—breeds habit. Try this and let me know how it goes.

The "Step Up 'n' Out" Section

Once you complete a meditation, you might have an action item you want to work on for yourself or for others. Something you want to follow through on. Don't be surprised if the meditation causes you to have an awareness of something you might not have previously considered, or perhaps something that was waiting for you to stand up and do or achieve.

Be. Become. The discoveries and action points of your ruminations can no longer take the backseat in the post-meditative you.

So, the "Step Up 'n' Out" section provides a place for however many action items you want to work on. Remember, keeping it simple is key. Whether it's something that requires immediate action on your part, or something that takes years to see the fruits of your intentional activities (if you're fortunate to live long enough to see the transformative change you initiate). Don't second guess or put off your "Step Up 'n' Out." Go ahead, make your day!

Motivate yourself.
Encourage yourself.
Activate yourself and take action today.

What If . . . 53 MEDITATIONS OF THE SOUL

THE MEDITATIONS

What if . . .

I matter

I matter

For real	Later

Step Up 'n' Out

I matter

For real	*Later*

Step Up 'n' Out

What if . . .

My thoughts matter

My thoughts matter

For real

Later

Step Up 'n' Out

My thoughts matter

For real	Later

Step Up 'n' Out

What if . . .

Life matters

Life matters

For real	Later

Step Up 'n' Out

Life matters

For real	Later

Step Up 'n' Out

What if . . .

I choose to be alive today

I choose to be alive today

For real

Later

Step Up 'n' Out

I choose to be alive today

For real	Later

Step Up 'n' Out

What if . . .

I am not alone

I am not alone

For real	Later

Step Up 'n' Out

I am not alone

For real	Later

Step Up 'n' Out

What if . . .

I dare to believe

I dare to believe

For real

Later

Step Up 'n' Out

I dare to believe

For real	Later

Step Up 'n' Out

What if . . .

I dare to try

I dare to try

For real	Later

Step Up 'n' Out

I dare to try

For real	*Later*

Step Up 'n' Out

What if . . .

I face my fears

I face my fears

For real	Later

Step Up 'n' Out

I face my fears

For real	Later

Step Up 'n' Out

What if . . .

I allow myself to cry

I allow myself to cry

For real

Later

Step Up 'n' Out

I allow myself to cry

For real

Later

Step Up 'n' Out

What if . . .

It's okay to laugh . . . at myself

It's okay to laugh . . . at myself

For real	Later

Step Up 'n' Out

It's okay to laugh . . . at myself

For real	Later

Step Up 'n' Out

What if . . .

It's okay to be right

It's okay to be right

For real	Later

Step Up 'n' Out

It's okay to be right

For real	*Later*

Step Up 'n' Out

What if . . .

It's okay to be wrong

It's okay to be wrong

For real	Later

Step Up 'n' Out

It's okay to be wrong

For real	Later

Step Up 'n' Out

What if . . .

It's okay to ask for help

It's okay to ask for help

For real	Later

Step Up 'n' Out

It's okay to ask for help

For real	Later

Step Up 'n' Out

What if . . .

It's okay to have a good day

It's okay to have a good day

For real	Later

Step Up 'n' Out

It's okay to have a good day

For real	Later

Step Up 'n' Out

What if . . .

It's okay to have a rough day

It's okay to have a rough day

For real	Later

Step Up 'n' Out

It's okay to have a rough day

For real	Later

Step Up 'n' Out

What if . . .

I recognize my tongue holds power to wound or
heal

I recognize my tongue holds power to wound or heal

For real	Later

Step Up 'n' Out

I recognize my tongue holds power to wound or heal

For real	Later

Step Up 'n' Out

What if . . .

I choose to listen with my heart

I choose to listen with my heart

For real

Later

Step Up 'n' Out

I choose to listen with my heart

For real

Later

Step Up 'n' Out

What if . . .

I admit I'm head trippin'

I admit I'm head trippin'

For real	Later

Step Up 'n' Out

I admit I'm head trippin'

For real	Later

Step Up 'n' Out

What if . . .

I am beyond sorry

I am beyond sorry

For real

Later

Step Up 'n' Out

I am beyond sorry

For real	Later

Step Up 'n' Out

What if . . .

I'm willing to say sorry and actually live it

I'm willing to say sorry and actually live it

For real	Later

Step Up 'n' Out

I'm willing to say sorry and actually live it

For real	Later

Step Up 'n' Out

What if...

There's less grey than I thought

There's less grey than I thought

For real	Later

Step Up 'n' Out

There's less grey than I thought

For real	Later

Step Up 'n' Out

What if . . .

There's a point of no return

There's a point of no return

For real

Later

Step Up 'n' Out

There's a point of no return

For real	Later

Step Up 'n' Out

What if . . .

I just stop

I just stop

For real

Later

Step Up 'n' Out

I just stop

For real	Later

Step Up 'n' Out

What if . . .

I try again

I try again

For real	Later

Step Up 'n' Out

I try again

For real	Later

Step Up 'n' Out

What if . . .

I shut my big mouth

I shut my big mouth

For real	Later

Step Up 'n' Out

I shut my big mouth

For real	Later

Step Up 'n' Out

What if . . .

I take a stand

I take a stand

For real	Later

Step Up 'n' Out

I take a stand

For real	*Later*

Step Up 'n' Out

What if . . .

I refuse to be part of the herd

I refuse to be part of the herd

For real	Later

Step Up 'n' Out

I refuse to be part of the herd

For real

Later

Step Up 'n' Out

What if . . .

I allow myself to be heard

I allow myself to be heard

For real

Later

Step Up 'n' Out

I allow myself to be heard

For real

Later

Step Up 'n' Out

What if . . .

I recognize the uniqueness of me

I recognize the uniqueness of me

For real

Later

Step Up 'n' Out

I recognize the uniqueness of me

For real	Later

Step Up 'n' Out

What if . . .

I say no

I say no

For real	Later

Step Up 'n' Out

I say no

For real	*Later*

Step Up 'n' Out

What if . . .

I say yes

I say yes

For real	Later

Step Up 'n' Out

I say yes

For real	Later

Step Up 'n' Out

What if . . .

I choose to be civil

I choose to be civil

For real	Later

Step Up 'n' Out

I choose to be civil

For real	Later

Step Up 'n' Out

What if . . .

I allow myself to wait

I allow myself to wait

For real

Later

Step Up 'n' Out

I allow myself to wait

For real	Later

Step Up 'n' Out

What if . . .

I let adrenaline lead

I let adrenaline lead

For real

Later

Step Up 'n' Out

I let adrenaline lead

For real

Later

Step Up 'n' Out

What if . . .

I take a spontaneous leap

I take a spontaneous leap

For real	Later

Step Up 'n' Out

I take a spontaneous leap

For real	*Later*

Step Up 'n' Out

What if . . .

I say something nice to a stranger

I say something nice to a stranger

For real	Later

Step Up 'n' Out

I say something nice to a stranger

For real	Later

Step Up 'n' Out

What if . . .

I step outside my comfort zone

I step outside my comfort zone

For real

Later

Step Up 'n' Out

I step outside my comfort zone

For real	Later

Step Up 'n' Out

What if . . .

I give generously

I give generously

For real

Later

Step Up 'n' Out

I give generously

For real	*Later*

Step Up 'n' Out

What if . . .

I enjoy life

I enjoy life

For real	Later

Step Up 'n' Out

I enjoy life

For real	Later

Step Up 'n' Out

What if . . .

I share my heart

I share my heart

For real	Later

Step Up 'n' Out

I share my heart

For real	Later

Step Up 'n' Out

What if . . .

I allow myself to fail

I allow myself to fail

For real

Later

Step Up 'n' Out

I allow myself to fail

For real	*Later*

Step Up 'n' Out

What if . . .

I allow myself to feel pain

I allow myself to feel pain

For real

Later

Step Up 'n' Out

I allow myself to feel pain

For real

Later

Step Up 'n' Out

What if . . .

I smile

I smile

For real

Later

Step Up 'n' Out

I smile

For real	*Later*

Step Up 'n' Out

What if . . .

I give hugs

I give hugs

For real	Later

Step Up 'n' Out

I give hugs

For real	*Later*

Step Up 'n' Out

What if . . .

I choose to forgive others

I choose to forgive others

For real

Later

Step Up 'n' Out

I choose to forgive others

For real

Later

Step Up 'n' Out

What if . . .

I admit no one is perfect

I admit no one is perfect

For real

Later

Step Up 'n' Out

I admit no one is perfect

For real	Later

Step Up 'n' Out

What if . . .

I forgive myself

I forgive myself

For real	Later

Step Up 'n' Out

I forgive myself

For real

Later

Step Up 'n' Out

What if . . .

I see at least one good thing in my "enemy" this day

I see at least one good thing in my "enemy" this day

For real	Later

Step Up 'n' Out

I see at least one good thing in my "enemy" this day

For real	Later

Step Up 'n' Out

What if . . .

I stop and hear myself think

I stop and hear myself think

For real

Later

Step Up 'n' Out

I stop and hear myself think

For real	Later

Step Up 'n' Out

What if . . .

I take 15 seconds to appreciate my surroundings

I take 15 seconds to appreciate my surroundings

For real	Later

Step Up 'n' Out

I take 15 seconds to appreciate my surroundings

For real	Later

Step Up 'n' Out

What if . . .

I do one thing to improve my surroundings

I do one thing to improve my surroundings

For real

Later

Step Up 'n' Out

I do one thing to improve my surroundings

For real	Later

Step Up 'n' Out

What if . . .

I love expecting nothing in return

I love expecting nothing in return

For real

Later

Step Up 'n' Out

I love expecting nothing in return

For real

Later

Step Up 'n' Out

What if . . .

I am responsible for my actions

I am responsible for my actions

For real	Later

Step Up 'n' Out

I am responsible for my actions

For real	Later

Step Up 'n' Out

FINAL THOUGHTS

Now that you've come through this meditation experience, I hope that among other things, you have discovered a way to easily and effectively meditate at your own pace and will continue to keep up the practice in a way that makes sense to you. Perhaps there are certain points you put down in the "Later" or "Step Up 'n' Out" portions of your meditation journey that are whispering to you to go back and further explore—to tease out whatever's calling to you to be teased out. So press on!

May *What If . . . 53 Meditations of the Soul* be a conduit to your finding moments of peace in the unsettled environment we face in our world today.

I encourage you to carry this book with you wherever your day may find you. See, the thing of meditating is that in chewing on something for a good long while, you extract all the goodness from that which you are thinking about. You will be struck by thoughts, ideas, and possibilities when you least expect it. By carrying this book with you, you will be able to ruminate freely whenever and wherever the idea comes to you. So do your thang and "chew your cud!"

MEDITATION REFERENCE LIST

ABOUT THE AUTHOR

Seeing people thrive and succeed in what they were created to do gives Waceke's heart joy. She loves people and stories, which turns out to be a natural progression to helping others, as evidenced in her childhood days and her more than 20-year career in healthcare. Both science and the creative find a ready and willing home in Waceke through her current focus as a voice actor, a podcaster, and an author. She loves her family deeply and is that crazy aunt who enjoys entering the realm of the impossibly possible world so readily championed by the little ones in our midst.

Connect with Waceke across social media where you can discover the latest happenings.

Instagram: @tataceke | LinkedIn: Waceke-Wambaa

Twitter: @tataceke | Website: tataceke.com

For one-on-one strategic coaching sessions with Waceke or for speaker inquiries, feel free to reach out at inquiries@tataceke.com.

Made in the USA
Columbia, SC
08 May 2023

16256855R00143